ITALIA

BRAVE EXPLORERS

REAL STORIES OF
BOLD JOURNEYS AND DISCOVERIES

Illustrations by Giulia Dragone
Text by Jacopo Donati

whitestar kids

Contents

Alexandra David-Néel
36
Annie "Londonderry" Kopchovsky
38
Robert O'Hara Burke and William John Wills
40
Nellie Bly
42
Mary Kingsley
44
Amelia Earhart
46
Roald Amundsen
48
Ernest Shackleton
50
Umberto Nobile
52
Charles Darwin
54
Yuri Gagarin
56
Edmund Hillary and Tenzing Norgay
58
Marie Tharp
60

Introduction

Hi! You've packed your backpack, right?

What you're holding in your hands are the stories of some of the explorers that came before you. You'll learn about the feats of men and women who had the courage to push beyond known frontiers. You'll find out everything you need to know to join the Explorers' Club, too.

I've selected only the most incredible stories: from Erik the Red, who discovered Greenland, to David Livingstone, who fought injustice in Africa, to Marie Tharp, who explored the ocean floors. Each one took on a new challenge, and there's no one better to show you what it means to be a real explorer. Some of them have even left you some words of encouragement!

You'll find not just dates and places, but emotions, lucky mistakes, extraordinary friendships, and discoveries that changed the world. Some explorers discovered unknown lands, others forged new paths for mankind, but all have taught us that curiosity is the most powerful compass we have.

I hope you've taken everything you need to travel the oceans, deserts, and mountains. You'll encounter far-off and surprising cultures, and at the end I'm certain you'll ask yourself: what's my next destination?

Anyway, enough procrastinating: it's time to set off!

Erik the Red and Leif Eriksson

The First Explorers of the North

In 960, at the age of ten, Erik the Red moved with his family from Norway to distant Iceland, which his great-great-uncle had actually discovered many years earlier.

When he grew up, he settled down, but Iceland started to suffocate him. What lands lay in wait for him beyond the sea? Erik gathered his family's things and they set sail to explore the seas. A few weeks later, they reached dry land and christened that place Greenland. They built a large camp because Erik had decided to put down roots, but not everyone wanted to stay.

One of Erik's sons was called Leif, and he loved the sea, too. Leif had heard a story he couldn't get out of his head: before reaching camp, very strong winds had pushed a ship beyond Greenland. On the horizon they had clearly made out a new and unexplored land.

What was there beyond those waves? Leif took a fast boat, and like his father had done before him (and his great-great-uncle even earlier!), explored the cold Arctic waters until he found what he was looking for. He called that land Vinland, which we now call Canada!

A BAD-TEMPERED CHARACTER

We don't know why Erik was called "the Red": perhaps he had red hair, or maybe he had... a fiery temperament! In fact, he was banished from Iceland for several years, having been accused of killing a neighbor after a terrible fight.

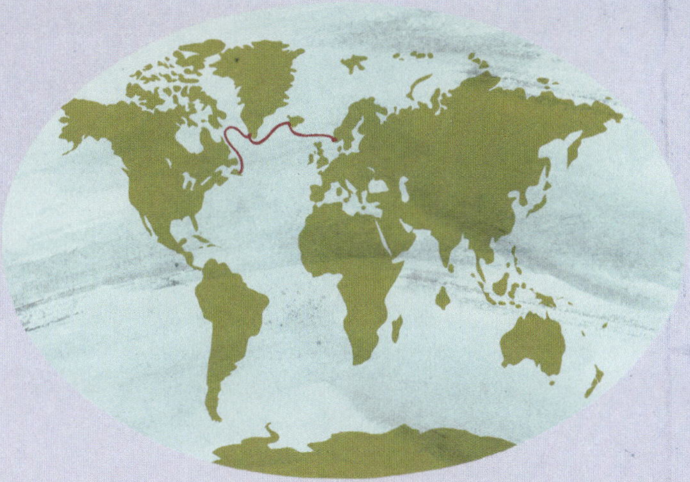

I will take my boat and find that land.

Leif didn't really know what lay in store, but his curiosity was so great that it gave him courage and helped him push beyond his limits.

Marco Polo

A World of Wonders

When he was just fifteen, Marco Polo set off on an incredible adventure with his father. They left Venice in 1271 and traveled along the Silk Road, an extremely long network of routes that would take them to distant Mongolia.

In Constantinople, Marco was captivated by the palaces. By contrast, in Armenia, he was struck by the high mountains. And what can we say about the perfumes of Baghdad? And the lapis lazuli of Badakhshan? He was fascinated by the people in particular, because they only needed to travel for a few days to encounter different cultures, new religions, and customs never seen before!

It took them four years, but one day they finally reached Mongolia. Marco quickly became friends with the great emperor Kublai Khan, who asked him to stay at court. His experience with foreign peoples would come in handy again, and Marco met the sovereigns of India, Vietnam, Sri Lanka...

He returned to Venice after spending twenty-four years in the Far East, and to all those who asked him if the stories he told were true, he would always answer: "I did not tell half of what I saw."

Read this book and you will discover the wonders of the peoples of Armenia, Persia, Mongolia, India...

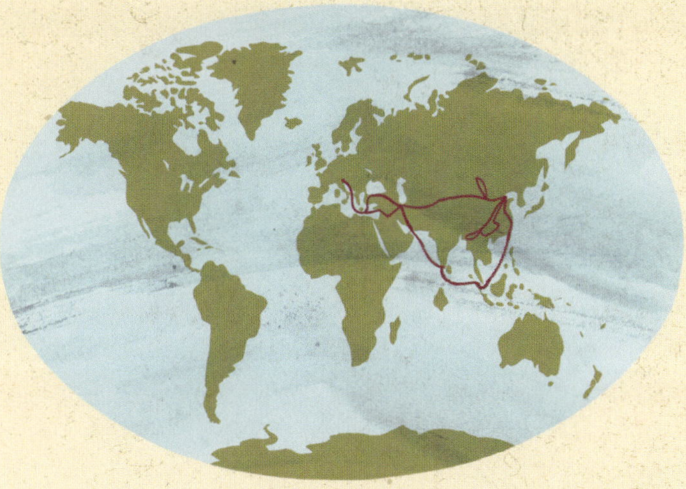

The book containing all his adventures is called *Il Milione* (which means "The Million"). Each page reminds us that all cultures have their own beauty, and learning about them helps us appreciate our own diversity.

A MILLION NEW THINGS

Aside from the stories, Marco Polo brought back many things to Europe that, at the time, were absolute novelties! One of these was banknotes, widely used in the Mongol Empire but completely unknown in Venice, where they still used gold and silver coins.

Zheng He

The Treasure Fleet

Zheng He lost his parents when he was a child, and in 1383 he became a servant to the Prince of Yan in northern China.

He and the prince were almost the same age, and so they developed a strong bond. The prince allowed him to study (a rarity at the time) and gave him increasingly more important assignments. The last one was the most incredible: they entrusted him with a fleet of 300 boats and a crew of 28,000 people! The instructions were clear: Zheng He had to show the world the wonders of China while collecting the most beautiful treasures and bringing them home. The Treasure Fleet was born! Zheng He sailed to Brunei and Java, then touched Thailand, Bangladesh, India, the Arab peninsula, the Horn of Africa... In every port he showed off the porcelain and silk China was famous for, and in return he bought everything: precious jewels and stones, spices and incenses, beautiful rugs, and even a giraffe!

The first voyage was such a success that the prince (now the emperor), replicated it not once, not twice, not three times, but... seven times!

AN ALMOST MYTHICAL ANIMAL

When he brought the giraffe he had bought in an African port to China, everyone thought it was a qilin, a mythical Chinese creature that was said to announce the birth of a great sage.

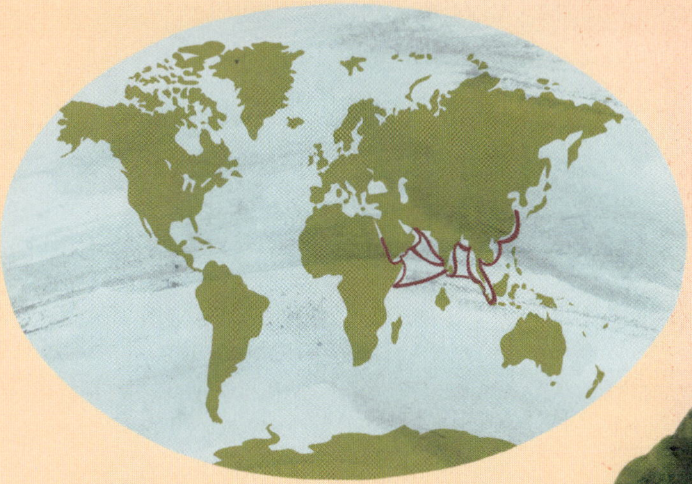

Every person you meet enriches two lives: yours and theirs.

During the seven voyages made by the Treasure Fleet, Zheng He got to know many people from different cultures from his own. These exchanges were more than business affairs, but rather an instrument of peace and reciprocal knowledge.

Christopher Columbus

A New Orient

European merchants had always used the Silk Road to reach Asia, but at the end of the fifteenth century, many wars complicated their journey. How to get to Asia? Christopher Columbus, an explorer from Genoa, had an idea!

At the time, people already knew that Earth was round, and if the route that went to the east was blocked, why not go from the other side, from the west? Columbus studied the maps, but none showed that side of Earth.

The king and queen of Spain provided him with three ships—the *Niña*, the *Pinta* and the *Santa María*—and in 1492 he set sail toward unexplored seas. His destination? Japan!

After weeks at sea, the crew was tired and wanted to turn back, but Columbus remained determined: they had to continue. And it was a good decision! One night a sailor shouted: “Land ahoy!” When they went ashore, the crew was welcomed by the Taíno tribe. The sailors were amazed to see people so different from them, with completely new customs and clothes.

It wasn’t Asia as Columbus had hoped, but a beautiful island that came to be known as San Salvador.

A FORTUNATE MISTAKE

Columbus had miscalculated and was convinced that Earth was much smaller. Just as well! In fact, at the time, ships couldn't carry enough supplies for such a long journey, and if the calculations had been correct, he might never have set sail. Never despair when you make a mistake: it might turn out to be a stroke of luck!

Columbus knew that this was a journey that no one had ever attempted before, but he could not have imagined that it would start a new chapter in human history. Sometimes our actions, no matter how big or small, can have incredible consequences!

I shall not go by land to the eastward, but I shall go by way of the west, whither up to this day, we do not know for certain that anyone has gone.

John Cabot

Ice-Bound Route

John Cabot, an explorer from Venice, had followed the exploits of Christopher Columbus with great interest. He was convinced that if he passed closer to the North Pole, he would find a passage to China.

Achieving that, however, wasn't so simple. In fact, the strong ocean currents pushed the ships toward the south, making the route Cabot wanted to take difficult. He couldn't leave from Spain like Columbus had done, but he had to go north, much farther north! And so he chose the port of Bristol in England.

The first expedition set sail in 1496, but he encountered bad weather from the outset, forcing them to return to port. However, he was not discouraged! The year after, he left again for North America.

Once again, he failed to find a passage to Asia. Still, his voyages weren't a total failure! In fact, his tenacity enabled him to find the first safe route to those lands and draw detailed maps of the coasts they encountered.

When he returned to England, the king celebrated him like a hero!

WHEN PASSION BEATS EXPERIENCE

John Cabot was a very resourceful man. Despite not having much sailing experience, in all likelihood it was his enthusiasm that convinced King Henry VII to finance his sea voyages.

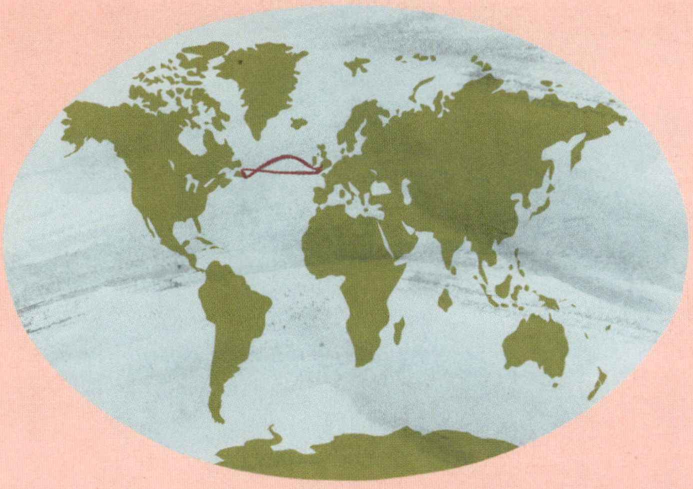

Hurdles don't kill a dream, but the fear of achieving it does.

John Cabot would have agreed with this statement: he knew that if he kept at it, he would succeed, and he wasn't discouraged by his early setbacks. Every mistake he made was a precious lesson he would learn.

Vasco da Gama

The Dangerous Monsoons

In 1497, Vasco da Gama left Lisbon with a highly ambitious goal: to complete the longest sea voyage ever achieved up to that point!

How long? Just think: the round trip would have been longer than the equator! Vasco was not unprepared, taking with him the most expert sailors he could find, as he needed skilled and brave souls.

From Lisbon he sailed along the coast of Africa, reaching the southernmost point of the continent, the Cape of Good Hope. Once there, the rest of the journey would be a breeze. Or perhaps not?

They stopped off in Mozambique, then Kenya. However, in Malindi, they dropped anchor because they risked sinking in the violent monsoons. No one had any experience in that bad weather, but Vasco asked for help from Kanji Malam, an Indian sailor who wasn't as famous as Vasco, but who had sailed through monsoons many, many times!

Thanks to his experience, they left Malindi behind and within a few weeks landed on the coast of India.

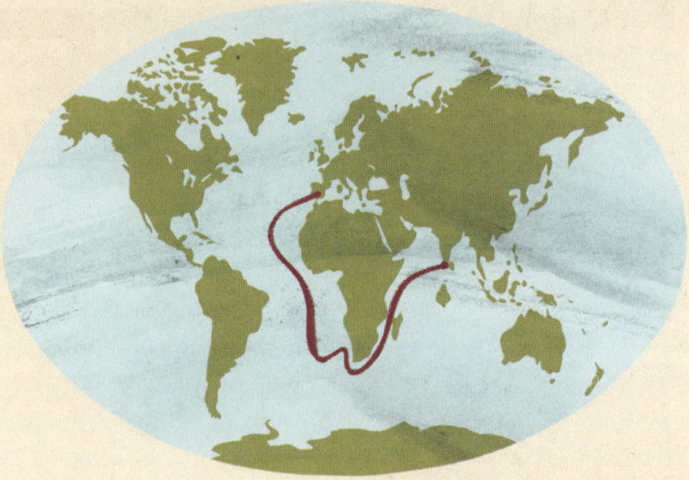

AN IMPATIENT EXPLORER

Vasco da Gama hated to be told no, and was often bad-tempered. One example was his bad behavior with the Indian merchants: when they refused to sell their goods at the low prices the Portuguese asked, Vasco actually went as far as to threaten them.

Amerigo Vespucci

The New World

In 1499, Amerigo Vespucci reached Brazil and crossed the vast mouth of the Amazon. He went down the coast where no European had ever reached, taking notes every day on everything he encountered. He realized that the plants he saw did not exist in any other known place. Even the people were very different from those who lived in Africa, Asia, or Europe. And what can we say about the beautifully colored birds that darted around in the sky?

Every observation convinced Amerigo even more that those places were not simply unexplored lands, but something different.

In fact, certain discoveries also need a moment of reflection to take shape! Amerigo reflected long and hard on what he'd seen, on the maps and the tales of other explorers, and in the end he arrived at a shocking conclusion: those lands were part of a New World, a new continent that had nothing to do with the known ones.

The cartographers who drew the maps of that continent decided to call it "America" in his honor!

A VERY AMBITIOUS AUTHOR

Amerigo Vespucci didn't come from a noble family, and this drove him to try and make contact with Spanish and Portuguese sovereigns. Becoming famous wasn't hard: his letters were so compelling that they quickly spread across Europe!

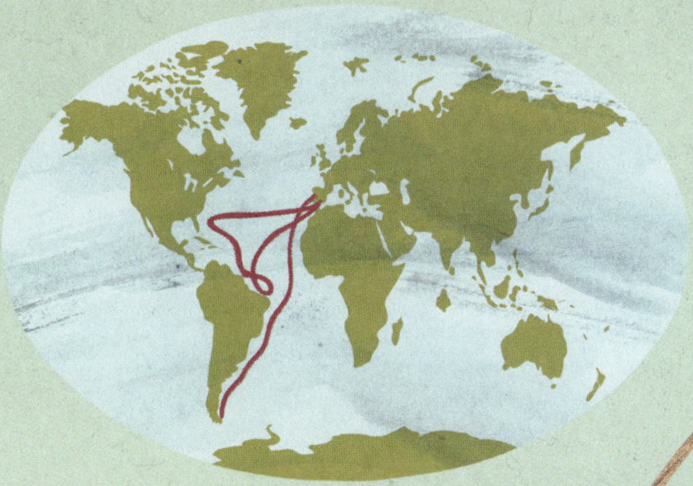

I had to study hard so I could understand with certainty the route we were following.

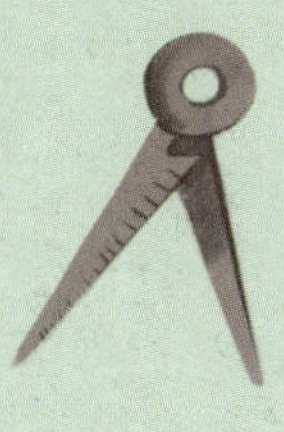

Amerigo knew full well that every journey carried huge risks, but studying them in depth meant he could face them with greater confidence!

Ferdinand Magellan

A Journey Around the Globe

In 1519, the king of Spain financed Ferdinand Magellan so that he could find a route that led to the current Maluku Islands. The well-known voyage passed the Cape of Good Hope, the southernmost point of Africa, but those seas were controlled by the Portuguese.

Magellan was certain there was an alternative route, perhaps close to South America. The idea was intriguing, but it would be a very long journey, the longest they had ever undertaken, and if they wanted to arrive safely, everything had to be carefully planned.

They started off from Seville and sailed to Brazil. They went along the coast until they found a long strait that, once crossed, finally brought them to the Pacific Ocean!

However, in the Philippines, Magellan died in a clash with some indigenous people. His objective had been so close! Juan Sebastián Elcano, one of the captains, took command, and thanks to Magellan's meticulous planning, he didn't just reach the Maluku Islands, but even further! He continued west until they reached Spain, thereby becoming the first expedition to circumnavigate Earth.

AN INTERPRETER ON BOARD

On board, there was also someone who spoke the language of their destination: Enrique, a young man from those parts, was brought along by Magellan so that he could negotiate the best prices with the spice merchants. He had really thought of everything!

Life is full of unexpected events, but if you are well prepared, you don't have to fear any obstacle.

The sea is perilous and storms terrible, but these obstacles have never been enough to leave me stranded.

Giovanni da Verrazzano

THE EXPLORER WHO MADE FRIENDS

In 1523, the king of France tasked Giovanni da Verrazzano with finding a passage that connected the Atlantic with the Pacific, and that the French could claim as their own. He left with a small ship and a few men, and after a few months glimpsed the headland we now called Cape Fear: now was the time to explore!

He described the coves, the rivers, and the large forests that covered those lands. He noted everything in a long letter to the king of France, and based on the accounts he made, it was immediately clear that one thing interested him in particular: people.

He often went ashore to meet the native peoples. He met the Lenape tribe aboard thirty canoes and received a delegation from the Wampanoag and Narragansett tribes. He was most struck by a group of indigenous people dressed in bird feathers who greeted them by screaming with joy!

After this incredible journey, Verrazzano explored the Caribbean islands. However, after the Bahamas and the island of Guadeloupe, all trace of him was lost. Who knows if he stayed for dinner with some local tribes...

We noticed a group of people coming to the seashore to look at us. We reassured them we were friends.

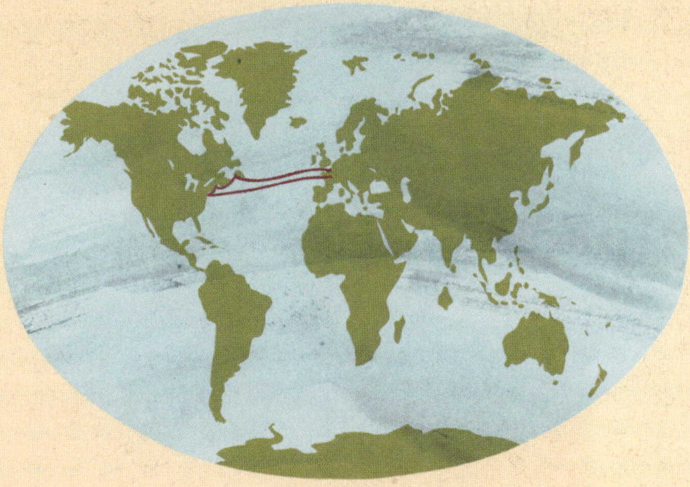

For Giovanni da Verrazzano, it was important that the people he met didn't feel threatened by him, but understood that his intentions were peaceful.

EXTRAORDINARY FRIENDS

Do you know who Verrazzano's neighbor was in Florence? Leonardo da Vinci! And in 1517, a few years after the famous voyage around the world, Verrazzano met Ferdinand Magellan in Lisbon. He really knew everyone!

Jeanne Baret

The Woman Who Circumnavigated Earth

If we've still not talked about female explorers, it's because in certain countries, like France, it was illegal for them to take part in an expedition!

Obviously, that didn't sit right with the naturalist Jeanne Baret, so in 1766, she disguised herself as a man and joined an expedition. She boarded the *Étoile* just before they weighed anchor, and before you knew it they were sailing out to sea. In Rio de Janeiro, she collected a plant with beautiful red flowers, which she named bougainvillea, and then minerals in Patagonia, shells, flowers... She collected more than 6,000 natural specimens on her own!

Her disguise was so good that for several months no one realized the truth. However, after disembarking in Tahiti, a group of indigenous people knew that Baret was a woman and revealed this to the rest of the crew. When they stopped off in Mauritius, the captain set off again and left her on land. No matter, though, because Baret continued her research in Madagascar and on Reunion Island.

When she finally set foot in Paris, she was the first woman to have circumnavigated Earth!

A LATE RECOGNITION

In 1785, the French navy guaranteed Baret a pension. Many years had passed since the *Étoile* set sail, but the courage and determination behind her feat were finally rewarded.

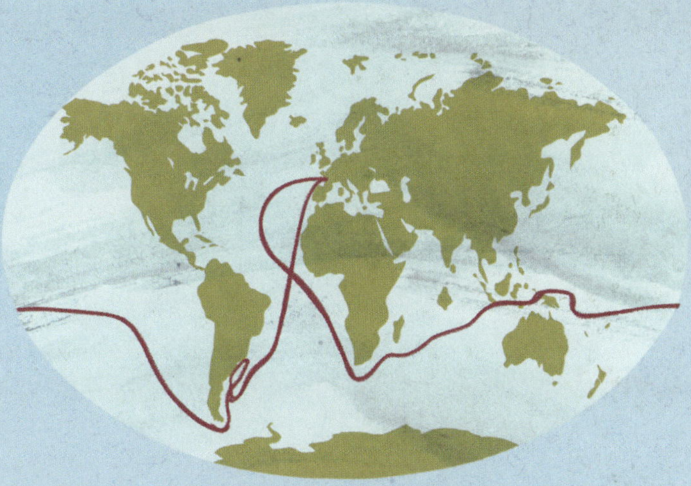

A PLANT DEDICATED TO HER

A plant she discovered in Madagascar was named *Baretia bonafidia* in her honor, but soon it turned out it had already been discovered. But in 2012, she was finally honored with a new plant named after her: *Solanum baretiae*.

James Cook

The Cartographer of the Seas

As a child, James Cook had one passion: the sea!

When he was a young man, he worked on a ship transporting coal. It wasn't an exciting job, but he learned everything about sailing, while in the evening he studied mathematics and astronomy. He got so good at drawing maps that the navy gave him increasingly important missions.

The opportunity Cook had been waiting for arrived in 1768, when he was given command of the *Endeavour* and an extraordinary mission: to find the mysterious "Terra Australis" in the South Pacific.

Cook left with scientists, artists, and sailors. They sailed south until a coast appeared on the horizon: it was New Zealand, and Cook carefully drew maps of the coasts and also discovered eastern Australia, which he called New South Wales. He circumnavigated the Antarctic, sketching every island and bay with extraordinary precision.

He died on the third voyage, during a fight with the indigenous people of Hawaii. He was fifty years old and had changed world geography for ever.

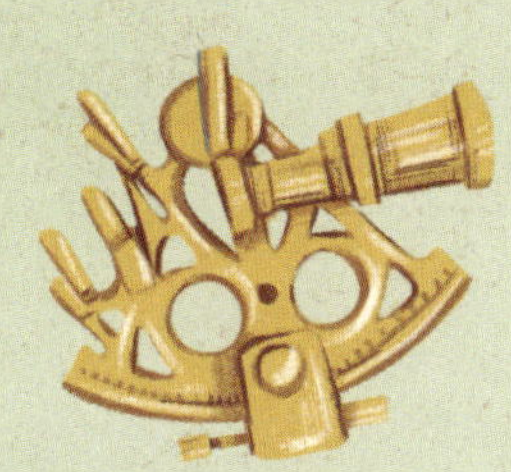

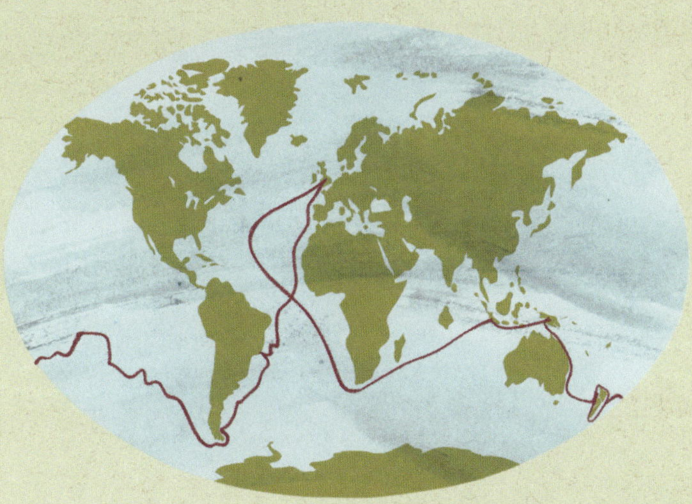

INCREDIBLE MAPS

The maps drawn by James Cook during his expeditions were so precise and detailed that they were used for many years, up to the twentieth century. They were only replaced by satellite images!

LIFE-SAVING LEMONS!

James Cook understood the importance of fresh food and citrus fruits in preventing scurvy, a terrible disease caused by a lack of vitamin C that often afflicted sailors, and no members of his crew got sick.

Jean-François de La Pérouse

The Mystery of the Pacific

In 1785, the king of France charged Jean-François de La Pérouse with exploring the most remote areas of the Pacific.

La Pérouse did not take the assignment lightly. He brought with him two sturdy ships, the *Boussole* and the *Astrolabe*, and a crew capable of studying everything they found: plants, animals, peoples, coasts...

He sailed the most perilous oceans for three years. He sailed along the coast of Alaska and California; he reached Hawaii, the Philippines, China, Japan, and Russia. He drew extremely detailed maps and sent his reports to France.

In 1788, he arrived in Sydney, Australia. He sent a letter with the route, then... no more news. What happened to Jean-François de La Pérouse? For a long time no one knew, but forty years later, some explorers found the remains of his ships near the island of Vanikoro, in the archipelago of the Solomon Islands: they had run into rocks in a severe storm and sank.

La Pérouse never returned home, but his maps and diaries arrived in France and helped generations of explorers.

AN ENLIGHTENED EXPLORER

In California, La Pérouse openly criticized the Spanish missions that treated the native Americans like slaves. He believed in the values of the French Enlightenment and that every person deserved dignity and rights.

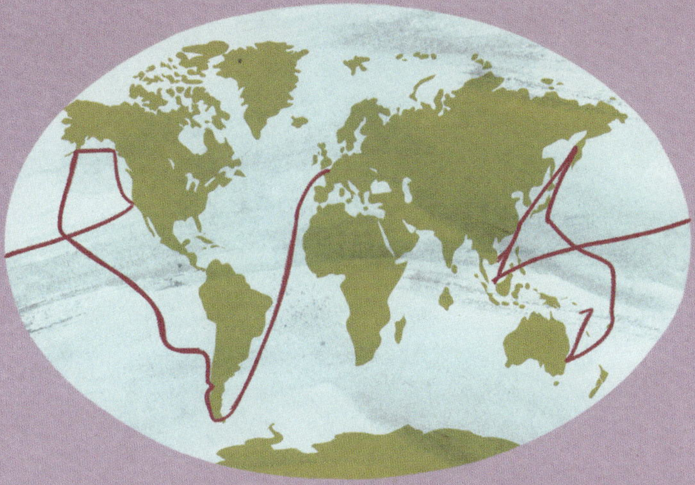

An enemy conquered should have nothing to fear; he then becomes a friend.

After capturing a British fort in Hudson Bay, La Pérouse left them enough supplies to survive the impending winter cold. He was a firm believer that after a conflict, we should always try to forge peace.

Alexander von Humboldt

The Baron Who Loved Nature

Alexander von Humboldt was born into a rich German family, but palaces bored him. He wanted to discover the secrets of nature!

In 1799, at the age of thirty, he left for South America with his friend Aimé Bonpland. They sailed along the Orinoco River in a small canoe, fighting off ferocious mosquitoes and hungry crocodiles. Humboldt took notes on everything: he measured the temperature of the water, he collected plants that intrigued him, he observed the stars at night. He never stopped!

In Ecuador he climbed the volcano Chimborazo, which at the time was considered the highest mountain in the world. Humboldt reached an altitude of over 16,400 feet (5,000 meters), where the air was so thin it was hard to breathe, but he kept measuring, taking notes, and studying.

Five years later, when he returned to Europe, he brought with him 60,000 different plants, more than 6,000 of which were unknown. He recounted what he had seen, becoming an inspiration for many people who understood the importance of protecting the nature that surrounds us.

A MULTIFACETED GENIUS

Humboldt was what you call a "multi-faceted genius," in other words, someone who is good at doing loads of different things. In fact, he wasn't just an explorer, but a botanist, meteorologist, writer, artist, and even philosopher!

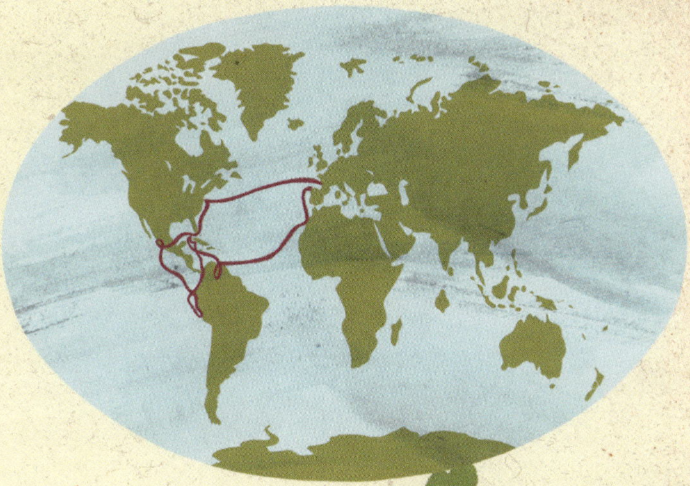

In the many books he wrote, he explained that everything in nature is connected: plants depend on the climate, animals on plants, and we depend on all of this.

I shall try to find out how the forces of nature interreact upon one another.

Lewis and Clark and Sacagawea

A Journey Through the Unknown

In 1804, two explorers named Meriwether Lewis and William Clark set out on an audacious mission: to map the vast lands of the American West and reach the Pacific Ocean. With them was Sacagawea, a young Shoshone woman who carried her infant son on her back, guiding the group across fast-flowing rivers, imposing mountains, and unknown lands.

Sacagawea was not just a translator, but a bridge between their cultures: she helped them trade with native tribes, find edible plants, and stay safe in dangerous lands. Her calmness showed the other tribes that the expedition was a peaceful one.

She walked thousands of miles, often barefoot, with her baby boy, Pompy, strapped to her back. When a boat risked capsizing, she saved diaries and maps from the water, and when they needed horses to cross the Rocky Mountains, she negotiated with the Shoshone, re-uniting with her long-lost brother. It was such an emotional moment that she wept with joy.

Lewis and Clark admired her strength. She never received any pay, but her contribution was invaluable. She helped shape the success of one of the most important expeditions in American history.

A CARTOGRAPHER AND... A MAMMOTH?

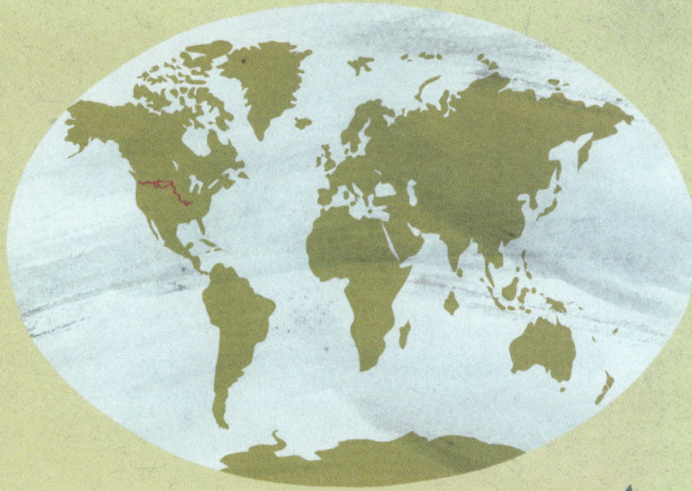

Before Lewis and Clark set out, President Thomas Jefferson believed they might encounter woolly mammoths, giant sloths, and even mountains of salt! The American West was so unknown that wild theories fueled the imagination. Although they didn't meet any prehistoric animals, the explorers discovered 178 new plants and 122 new animals, including coyotes, mountain goats, and grizzly bears.

The world is my country and all mankind are my brethren.

Their story reminds us that courage can take many forms and that even the quietest voices can show the way.

David Livingstone

The Doctor Who Fell in Love with Africa

David Livingstone was a young Scotsman with a big dream: to become a doctor and help people. To make it happen, he worked in a factory by day and spent his evenings studying.

In 1841, he left for Africa as a missionary and became fascinated with exploring unknown lands. He learned the local languages and made friends with African tribes. With his bag of medicines, he crossed deserts and forests. He discovered rivers, lakes, and spectacular waterfalls. He decided to name the most impressive one Victoria Falls in honor of Queen Victoria. However, the mission closest to his heart was helping people who were sold as slaves. Then, all traces of him were lost...

In 1871, when an English journalist finally managed to catch up with him, he found him debilitated by malaria. The journalist begged him to return home to heal, but it was useless: Livingstone was only going to leave Africa when his mission was complete.

Upon his death, two years later, his heart was buried at the foot of a baobab, so that he could always stay in the continent he loved so much.

AN EMBARRASSING IMAGE!

In 1844, Livingstone tried to drive away a lion by firing his gun, but he only enraged the lion even more! The image of the attack was published in a travel book, and Livingstone, embarrassed, was hoping that no one saw it: but unluckily for him, the book sold 70,000 copies!

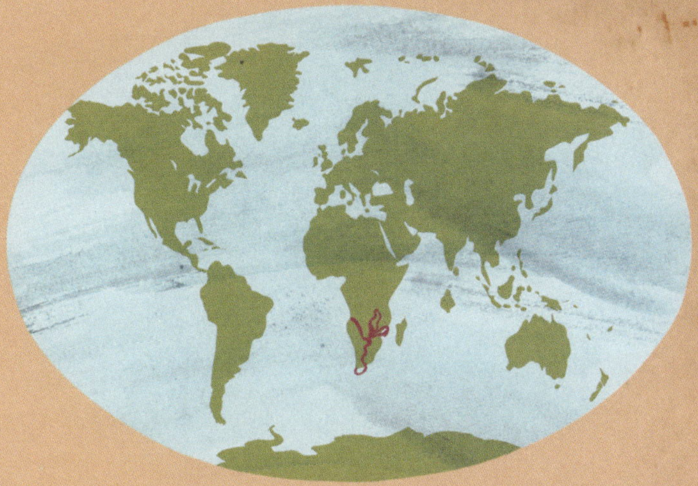

The more time he spent in Africa, the more he became aware of the suffering caused by slavery. The books he wrote on this topic changed many people's opinions!

May Heaven's rich blessing come down on everyone who will help heal slavery, an open sore of the world.

Alexandra David-Néel

A French Woman on the Roof of the World

Alexandra David-Néel had always been fascinated by eastern philosophies, so in 1911 she decided to set off for India. Her objective, however, lay among the mountains farther north.

Nestled among high mountains and dotted with ancient monasteries, this region was little known at the time. Alexandra met a monk called Yongden, and together they headed toward the capital, Lhasa. But the problem was foreigners were prohibited from entering! She learned the language, dressed like the local pilgrims, and, in 1924, entered Lhasa, mixing with the crowd who were celebrating a Buddhist festival.

Once inside, she wanted to snap a few photos, but didn't want to stand out as a foreigner. However, her disguise aroused someone's suspicion, who complained about her to the governor, but before he could do anything, she had already fled to a city nearby!

She returned to France after fourteen years of traveling, and for the rest of her life she never stopped talking about those incredible places!

TELEPATHIC MESSAGES

While she was traveling, she studied with some exceptional masters. No matter how strange it seemed, David-Néel was absolutely convinced that, on more than one occasion, her masters had sent her messages telepathically, that is via thought.

I believe that there is no better source of youth than these two things combined: traveling and studying.

Always discovering new things, either while traveling or in the pages of a book, arouses a sense of wonder in us that keeps us young. You can trust the opinion of David-Néel: she lived to one hundred!

Annie "Londonderry" Kopchovsky

Around the World on the Saddle of a Bicycle

In 1894, when girls had to wear long skirts and people said adventure didn't suit them, Annie Kopchovsky decided to show the opposite. She wore pants, got on a bike, and started out on a trip around the world!

Her bike was decorated with a small flag and symbols of the cities she visited, like a travel diary on two wheels. She wore a jacket with shiny golden buttons and a cyclist's cap that made her look both elegant and funny.

Her journey began in Boston in the United States, with just a few dollars in her pocket. In order to obtain sponsorship, she changed her surname to "Londonderry," from the name of a mineral water company who offered to support her. Kopchovsky pedaled during the day and regaled people with her stories at night, attracting throngs of curious onlookers wherever she went.

She traveled through Europe, Asia, the Middle East, and returned to America. It wasn't always plain sailing: she faced dangerous roads and strange languages, and she often just made up stories to entertain the public!

THE START OF A TWO-WHEELED REVOLUTION

Kopshovsky didn't even know how to ride a bike up until a few weeks before setting off! It didn't take her long to learn, and with courage and a great sense of humor, she became the first woman to travel around the world on a bike.

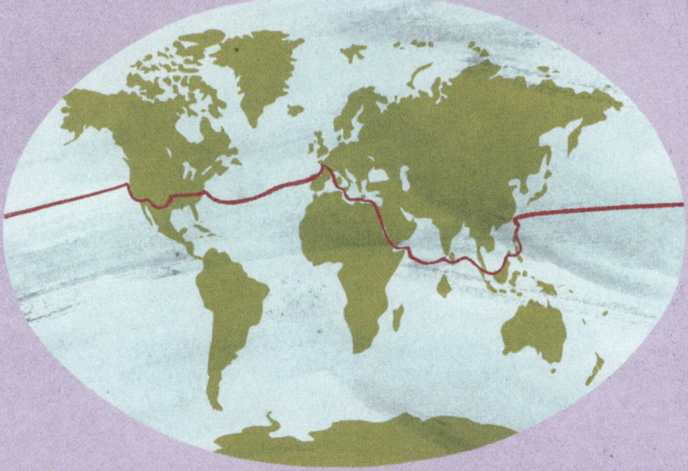

I am a journalist and a new woman, if that term means I think I can do anything a man can do.

It was a powerful message in her time and is still a source of inspiration today. With imagination and determination, Kopshovsky showed that a young woman could be an explorer, a traveler, and a true pioneer of adventure.

Robert O'Hara Burke and William John Wills

The Great Australian Traverse

In 1860, still no one had crossed Australia: Robert O'Hara Burke and William John Wills set their minds on being the first!

Burke was a brave but impatient police officer. Wills was an intelligent and meticulous young scientist. Together they headed up an expedition of nineteen men, twenty-six camels, and horses laden with supplies.

They left Melbourne in the dead of winter, reaching Cooper Creek in the summer, more or less the halfway point. They should have waited until autumn to set off again, but Burke was impatient, so he, Wills, and a few others continued northward: they crossed scorching deserts where it never rained and endless red earth plains.

In the summer of 1861, they finally reached the Gulf of Carpentaria! They'd done it! But the return journey was terrible. Food was in short supply and the monsoons slowed them down. When they arrived at base camp, it was empty: their companions had set off again just a few hours earlier.

When the rescue mission reached them, for Burke and Wills it was already too late.

THE WISDOM OF THE ABORIGINES

The only member of the expedition to be saved was an assistant who asked the Yandruwandha, the Aboriginal people, for help. The Aborigines had lived in those places for centuries, and if Burke and Wills had relied more on the knowledge of the local peoples, they would probably have been saved.

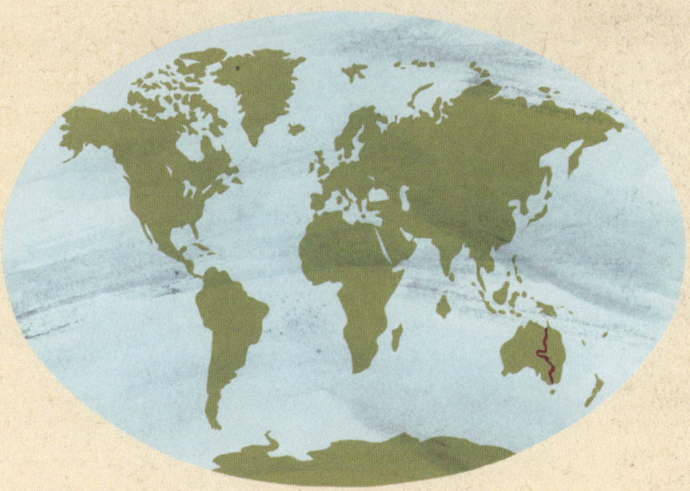

A DANGEROUS PLANT

At the end of the journey, there was little food, so Burke and Wills often ate a plant called nardoo. The Aborigines ate it, too, but only after cooking it: when eaten raw, it actually prevents the absorption of vitamin B1, and this was one of the causes of their deaths.

Nellie Bly

AROUND THE WORLD IN 72 DAYS

Nellie Bly was a young American journalist with a crazy dream: she wanted to travel around the world faster than anyone else! In 1889, everyone knew Jules Verne's book *Around the World in Eighty Days*, but Nellie was convinced she could do even better.

On November 14, she left from New York with a small bag. No enormous trunks, no servants: she was the first woman to travel completely solo!

She crossed the Atlantic Ocean to England, then continued toward France, where she met Jules Verne, the famous author. She took steam ships, trains, railroad-cars, and even rickshaws. She never stopped! Italy, Egypt, then on to Sri Lanka and Singapore. In China, she bought a small monkey, who accompanied her on the rest of her journey. In Japan, another ship brought her to America, while the whole world followed her adventures in the newspapers.

Readers waited for news every day: has she done it?

On January 25, 1980, she finally arrived in New York. It took her just 72 days, 6 hours, and 11 minutes!

JOURNALIST AND... INVENTOR!

The intelligence she had shown on her long voyage around the world was on show again once she'd returned home: she patented a milk can and stackable garbage containers!

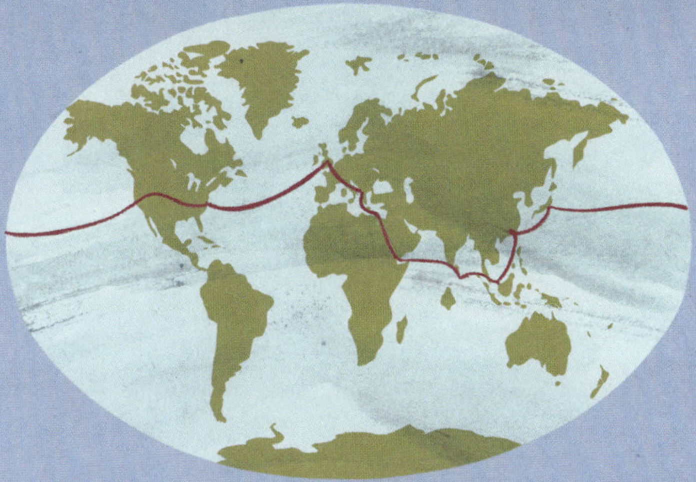

I have never written a word that did not come from my heart. I never shall.

Bly had always been occupied by matters close to her heart and thought everyone should know more. Also for this reason, her studies influenced a lot of people's opinions.

Mary Kingsley

THE HIDDEN TREASURES OF AFRICA

When she was young, Mary Kingsley loved to pass the days away in her father's library. She preferred the stories from far-off countries. In 1893, when she finally had the opportunity to travel, she chose the continent that fascinated her the most: Africa!

She arrived in Sierra Leone on a boat, and from there went on to the city of Luanda, in Angola. She was taken in by local people, who taught her how to survive in the most dangerous wilderness. During her travels, she encountered enormous bad-tempered hippos and ravenous crocodiles, but also crystal clear lakes and beautiful little islands covered in vegetation.

Whenever she could, she collected samples to bring back to England, like fish, plants, and insects. She also collected people's stories, and each encounter convinced her that Africa and the people that inhabited it were a treasure that should be protected and understood.

After getting back to England, she recounted her adventures in books that became really famous, showing how rich and diverse the African continent was.

A PRACTICAL SPIRIT

There was often something broken in the family home, because neither Kingsley's father nor mother took care of things. So she subscribed to a DIY magazine so she could carry out all the necessary repairs herself!

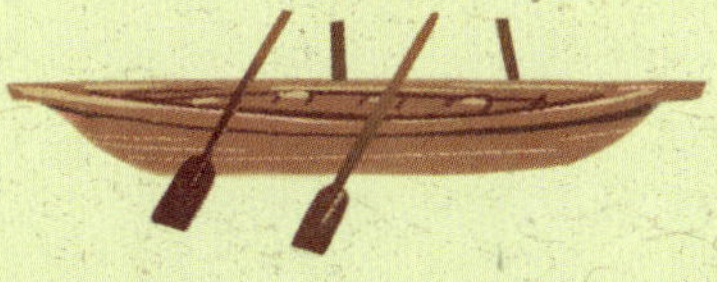

I am not one of those who will ever tell you things are impossible.

Kingsley didn't like the way many Europeans treated the peoples of Africa, and she hoped to change people's opinions with her books. The most important thing, when we are faced with a difficult endeavor, is to have the confidence that it can be done.

Amelia Earhart

FLYING TOWARD THE HORIZON

When she was twenty years old, Amelia Earhart took her first flight in an airplane and realized the sky would be her home.

In 1928, she was the first woman to cross the Atlantic Ocean as a passenger, then in 1932 was the first woman to cross the United States without a stop-over, i.e., in a single flight. However, for her that wasn't enough: her dream was to fly around the world!

It would have been an extremely long flight and she would have flown along the equator for 29,000 miles (47,000 kilometers)! She modified an airplane to ensure the maximum fuel tank capacity and carefully planned the journey to be sure she always had enough fuel.

On June 1, 1937, Earhart took off with her navigator, together crossing South America, Africa, India, and Southeast Asia. After arriving in Papua New Guinea, she only had a few legs before returning home: they took off for Howland Island, but they disappeared...

No one really knows what happened that day, and the remains of the aircraft were never found. Her courage, however, has never been forgotten.

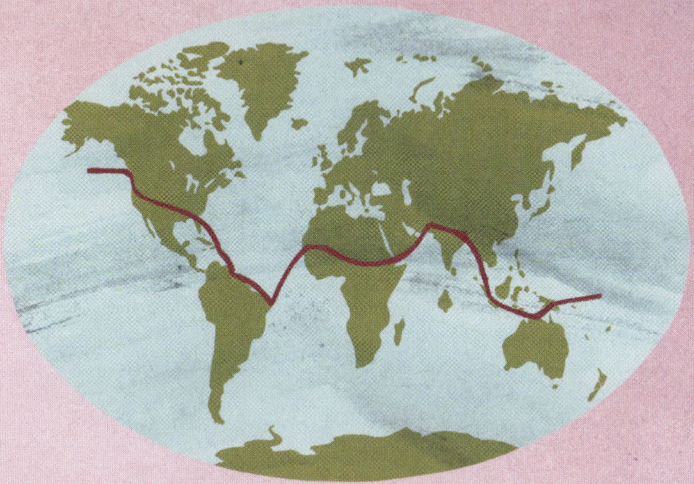

The most difficult thing
is the decision to act.
The rest is merely tenacity.

Earhart knew full well that when starting out on any undertaking it's easy to be paralyzed by fear. You just need the courage to start, and the rest will be easier.

EARHART'S VERY FIRST FLIGHT

Earhart's first flight was... in a wooden box! At the age of seven, with her uncle's help, she built a small roller coaster. However, during the first ride, the box she was sitting in broke apart and she flew out. Do you think she was scared? Not at all, she wanted an even taller roller coaster!

Roald Amundsen

Conqueror of the Poles

When he was a young boy, Roald Amundsen read the stories of explorer John Franklin and his extremely courageous Arctic expeditions. That's when he decided that, when he grew up, he'd explore the coldest regions on Earth!

In his first major feat in 1903, he sailed through the Northwest Passage, navigating the sea ice of Canada from the Pacific to the Atlantic. It took three years, but Amundsen was patient and prepared.

His ultimate ambition, however, was to reach the South Pole, the southernmost point on Earth, where no one had ever set foot! In 1911, he reached the Bay of Whales, on the coast of Antarctica. They were a party of four and had sleds pulled by dogs and supplies for weeks. Every day, they slipped on the snow for hours and hours, with temperatures of minus forty degrees Fahrenheit (minus forty degrees Celsius)!

The journey was extremely tough: deep crevices, blinding snowstorms, a cold that froze your breath. Danger was always just round the corner, but on December 14, 1911, Amundsen planted the Norwegian flag on the South Pole. He was first there!

A TOUGHENED PHYSIQUE

Even as a child, Amundsen knew that to be an explorer you needed to be in good shape. After school, he would explore the woods and the mountains to build up his muscles, and in winter he slept with the windows open wide to get used to the cold winds in the Poles. He had clear ideas!

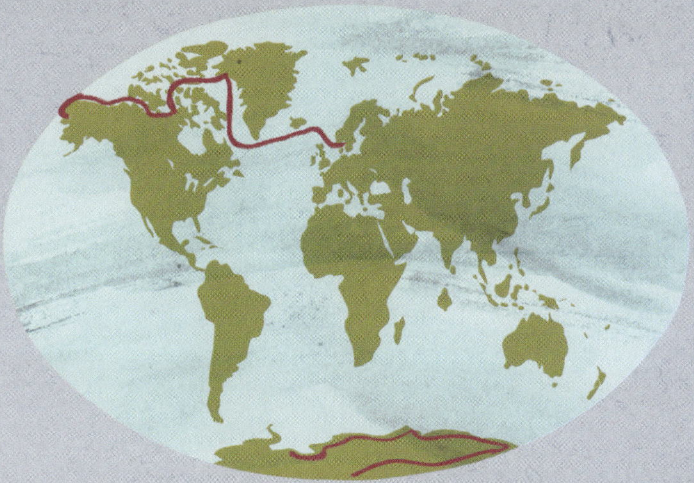

One of the reasons his expedition to the South Pole was a success was that Amundsen had planned everything in meticulous detail and was prepared for the unexpected. Some people call it luck, he called it being prepared!

Victory awaits him who has everything in order, luck, people call it.

Ernest Shackleton

THE INCREDIBLE JOURNEY OF THE *ENDURANCE*

Ernest Shackleton was an Irish explorer who organized an extraordinary expedition in 1914: to cross the Antarctic on foot, from one side to the other!

He set off on board the *Endurance* with twenty-seven men, but the Antarctic had other ideas: the ice crushed the ship like a giant clamp, trapping them for nearly a year. Then, one terrible day, the ship sank, and Shackleton and his men escaped in three lifeboats.

They remained on the ice for several months, thousands of miles from civilization, but Ernest did not lose heart. One day they put the lifeboats back into the sea and rowed to Elephant Island: it was a desolate place but at least it was dry land!

However, the real adventure had yet to begin. With one lifeboat and five men, Shackleton crossed 810 miles (1,300 kilometers) of storm-swept ocean, reaching South Georgia. It took them sixteen days, but they got there!

They sent help back straight away to their stranded companions, and almost two years after leaving they were all saved!

They hadn't made it across the Antarctic, but he had completed an even bigger feat: saving every member of his crew.

UNUSUAL INTERVIEWS

For Shackleton, the most important qualities of an explorer were optimism, patience, physical shape, idealism, and courage. That's why, during interviews, he asked questions to gauge candidates' character, not just their skills. He knew that the journey would be long and it was important for everyone to be on the same page.

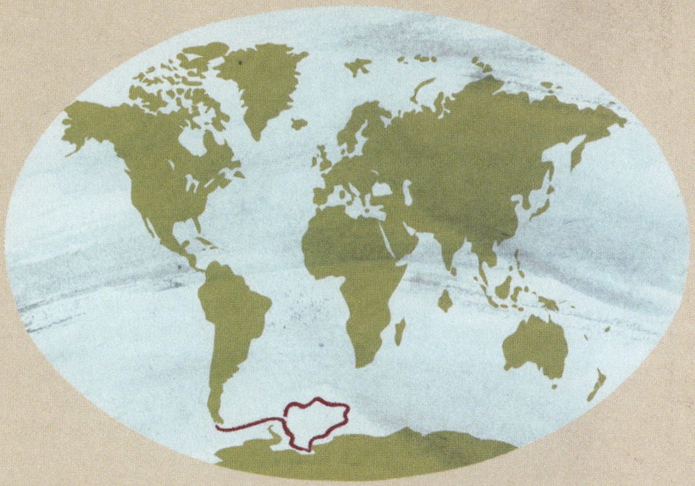

Difficulties are just things to overcome, after all.

We encounter difficulties in any adventure, but they shouldn't discourage us: once they've been overcome, we realize that we had nothing to worry about.

Umberto Nobile

Flying Over the Ice

Umberto Nobile was an Italian engineer who built airships, enormous flying hot air balloons that could travel thousands of miles. However, Nobile didn't want to just build them: he wanted to pilot them to the most remote places on Earth!

In 1926, he and Roald Amundsen reached the North Pole on his airship *Norge*. However, this wasn't enough: Nobile wanted to explore the entire Arctic! So, two years later, he set off on a new expedition on the airship *Italia*: loaded with scientific instruments, they drew maps and noted everything they saw. It was a success!

During the return journey, however, the airship lost altitude and plummeted onto the ice. Nobile and several men remained trapped on the pack ice, injured and with few supplies, but they didn't lose heart: they constructed a red tent so they were visible from the air and transmitted radio signals to seek help.

After nearly a month on the ice, their tenacity was finally rewarded, and a rescue mission brought them home!

A BRAVE PUPPY

Nobile had a puppy who never left his side: a fox terrier called Titina who shared the same indomitable spirit as her owner. A day after the incident, they heard her barking furiously: she was chasing away a polar bear who had gotten too close to their camp!

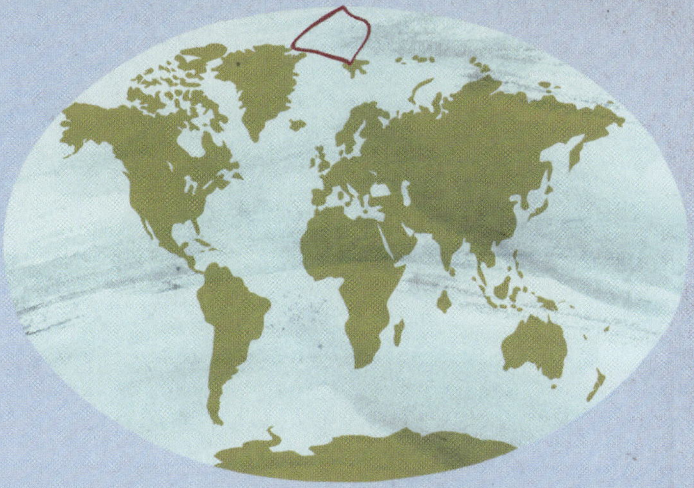

The risk lay in the fact that we were the first to attempt it. Being pioneers is an honor that comes at a price.

You have to be aware that being the first to do something comes with risks.

Charles Darwin

The Discovery of Evolution

Around 200 years ago, a young Englishman by the name of Charles Darwin set sail on a ship called *Beagle* to explore the world. The journey lasted almost five years, during which Darwin observed everything with great curiosity: animals, plants, fossils, and landscapes he had never seen before.

Darwin always brought with him a magnifying glass, a leather bag filled with instruments and samples, and a broad-brimmed hat to protect him from the hot tropical sun. He'd often sit by the sea taking notes in his journal resting on a trunk. He drew birds with strange beaks, gigantic tortoises, and all the little things that helped him understand how living creatures adapted to their environment.

His journey to the Galápagos Islands forever changed the way people viewed the natural world. After returning to England, he wrote a book in which he explained his discovery: animals hadn't always stayed the same, they had evolved!

WHEN A WEAKNESS LEADS TO A DISCOVERY!

As a child, Darwin wanted to study medicine, but he fainted at the sight of blood! Well, what seemed at first to be a weakness, proved to be a stroke of luck: thanks to that fear, Darwin chose a completely different path... and ended up changing science forever!

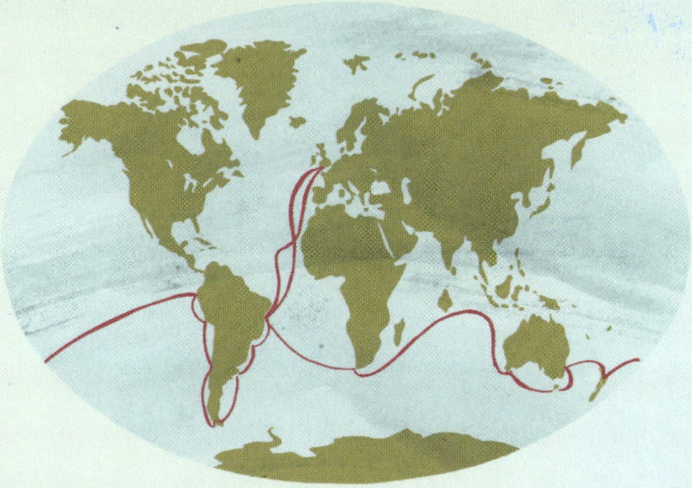

It is not the strongest of the species that survives. It is the one that is the most adaptable to change.

A profound insight that opened new horizons for science. Thanks to his yearning to understand and the true patience of an explorer, Darwin helped the world understand a wonderful secret: how the diversity of life on Earth is created.

Yuri Gagarin

The First Man in Space

Yuri Gagarin was a Russian pilot who was chosen from thousands to become a cosmonaut. He trained hard for several months: he had to get used to living in extremely confined spaces, dealing with rapid acceleration and zero gravity.

The big day arrived on April 12, 1961. Gagarin boarded *Vostok 1*, a small space shuttle that resembled a metallic sphere. When the engines fired up, the rocket started to tremble and it took off with a deafening thunder. Gagarin was squashed against the chair by the tremendous force of acceleration, but his training had prepared him for this!

It took just a few minutes for *Vostok 1* to leave Earth's atmosphere. Gagarin peered out the small window, observing a spectacle that no human being had ever seen before: Earth from space! A blue and white planet floating in the infinite darkness.

Gagarin orbited Earth for 108 minutes, then re-entered the atmosphere with a cloud of flames surrounding the space shuttle. He landed safe and sound in a field in Russia. He had become the first space explorer and forged a new frontier for mankind!

A REBELLIOUS YOUTH

In 1942, Gagarin's village was occupied by Nazi soldiers. He was a young boy, but that didn't mean he did nothing to slow them: when the soldiers were distracted, he stuffed the mufflers of their trucks with potatoes, so the trucks couldn't start up again.

I saw how beautiful our planet is. Let's preserve this beauty, and not destroy it!

Those who have had the fortune of gazing upon Earth from space are struck by the beauty and the fragility of our planet. It's easy to forget, but this is our home and it's our duty to protect it.

Edmund Hillary and Tenzing Norgay

On Top of the World

In 1953, two brave men set out to do what no one had done before: reach the summit of Mount Everest, the highest mountain in the world! One of them was Edmund Hillary, a beekeeper and mountaineer from New Zealand. The other was Tenzing Norgay, a Sherpa guide born at the foot of the Himalayas. Together, they made the perfect team: strong, able, and ready to take on the wind, snow, and freezing cold.

They wore heavy suits, big boots, and oxygen masks. On Hillary's backpack there was a small flag and a photo of his family. Tenzing carried a small statue in honor of the mountain spirits. After days of grueling climbing, with very little oxygen and exhausted, they finally reached the summit! They were at 29,030 feet (8,848 meters), above the clouds. An incredible feat!

Thanks to their courage and friendship, Hillary and Tenzing proved that the impossible can become reality. They showed deep respect for the mountain and for local traditions, and became explorers of the highest summit on Earth.

People do not decide to become extraordinary. They decide to accomplish extraordinary things.

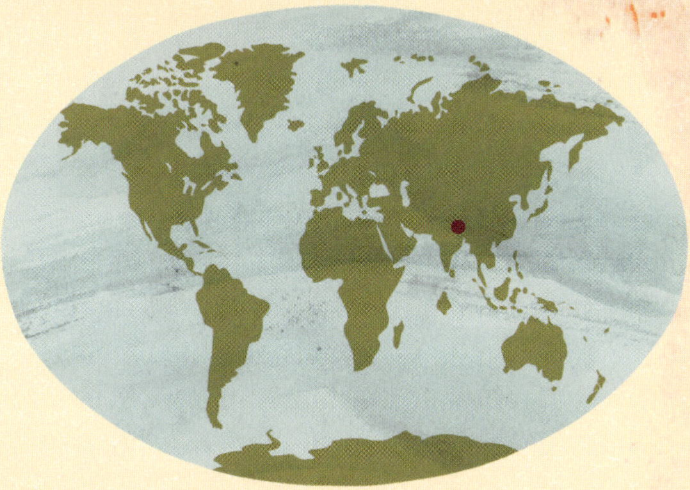

A phrase that reminds us that courage lives inside all of us.

HIGH-ALTITUDE FLAGS OF PEACE

At the top of Everest, Tenzing planted the flags of Nepal, India, the United Kingdom, and the United Nations to symbolize peace between nations. And guess what? Hillary took only one photo, of Tenzing, because he was too excited to get in the picture himself!

Marie Tharp

Explorer of the Ocean Floors

Marie Tharp was a young American fascinated by geography, but in the 1940s, women weren't allowed to board research ships!

In 1948, she started to work with geologist Bruce Heezen. He sailed the ocean collecting data using sonar, an instrument for measuring sea depth. Tharp instead remained on land and turned those numbers into maps. It was a laborious task, but little by little she discovered something extraordinary: there was an enormous submerged mountain chain in the middle of the Atlantic Ocean, the Mid-Atlantic Ridge!

Tharp continued her work for several decades. She drew maps of all the world's oceans: Atlantic, Pacific, Indian. Her drawings showed high underwater mountains and extremely deep canyons, volcanoes, and plateaus concealed by the sea.

Her maps revolutionized science and were proof that the continents move. Tharp had explored 70 percent of the planet, which had always remained hidden to human beings, and all this without ever getting on board a ship!

A GENUINE ALL-ROUND EXPERT

Tharp had loads of interests! At university she studied geography and cartography, as well as German, physics, history, mathematics, Latin, zoology, philosophy, paleobotany, art, chemistry, biology, and geology. If she could have, she would have majored in... everything!

One day Tharp was dismissed by the laboratory she worked for, but her only concern was finishing the map. Focused on the project, she started to work from home, and in no time her research was financed by the US Navy.

We had work to do and we pressed ahead.

Now we've come to the end of this extraordinary journey!

You have gotten to know some truly incredible characters and seen them cross oceans, deserts, and mountains. Their courage also forged new paths for all of us, too.
And now, guess what? The story of exploration is not over, it has actually just begun: it's your turn!

Our planet still hides innumerable secrets waiting for an explorer brave enough to discover them. In the depths of the oceans live creatures never seen before, the forests have plants with mysterious properties, and space is a frontier packed full of surprises. Who knows what's hidden beneath the earth's crust... Have you already decided where you want to start?

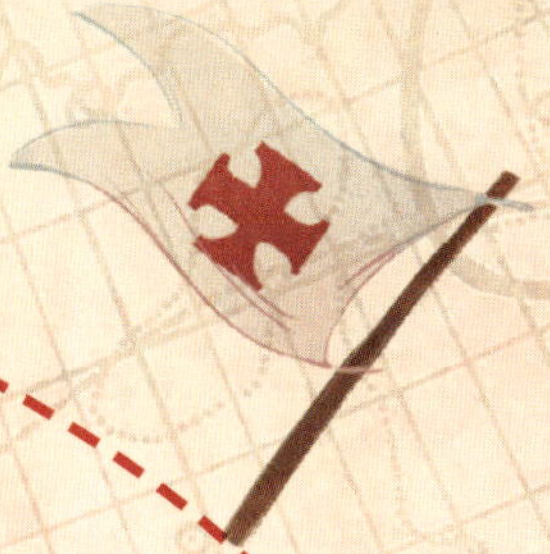

Remember that you don't need to travel far to be a real explorer. You can even start from where you are right now: ask questions, look for answers, and try lots of new things. Curiosity is the real inspiration for every adventure.

The explorers you've learned about in these pages were just normal people like you: they, too, were afraid and made mistakes, but they never let this stand in their way. What adventure awaits you?

Get ready: the world needs your curiosity and your courage. Bon voyage!

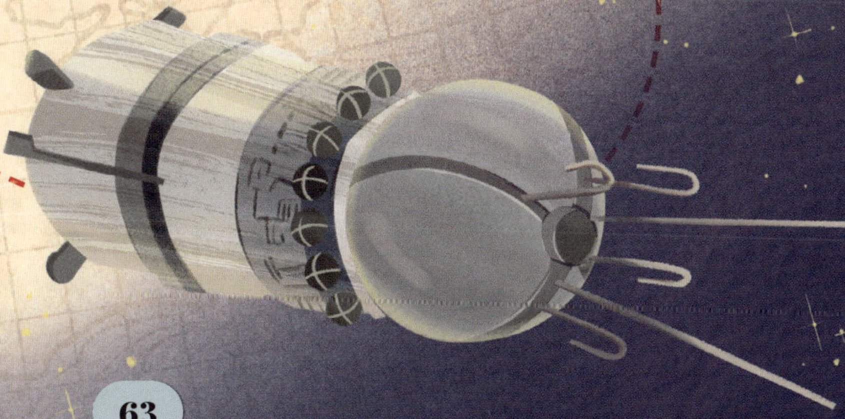

Giulia Dragone is an Italian illustrator and visual designer. With a degree in communication design, she has collaborated with various publishing houses, specializing in children's illustrations. Her colorful and detailed style captivates young readers, making every page a visually engaging experience.

Jacopo Donati is an editor and writer specializing in fiction. Formerly also a television writer, he now focuses exclusively on genre fiction and children's literature. He teaches editing and creative writing at Bottega Finzioni in Bologna, Italy, where he helps aspiring authors perfect their stories.

Design: Sara Travain

Piazzale Luigi Cadorna, 6 - 20123 Milan, Italy
www.whitestar.it

Translation: Qontent
Editing: Abby Young

First printing, October 2026

ISBN 978-88-544-2231-5
1 2 3 4 5 6   30 29 28 27 26

Printed and manufactured in China by
Shenzhen Dream Colour Printing Company Limited,
Shenzhen, Guangdong

FSC
www.fsc.org
MIX
Paper | Supporting responsible forestry
FSC® C178000